Tooney

The Cat Who Loved Music

Other Children's Books
By Julie Ronci Sipes
Illustrated by David Lawter:

The Wonderful World of Trees!

CHB Media, Publisher

Tooney
The Cat Who Loved Music

By Julie Ronci Sipes

Published by CHB Media

Copyright 2021 © Julie Ronci Sipes

All Rights Reserved

including the right of reproduction,

copying, or storage in any form

or means, including electronic,

in whole or part,

without prior written

permission of the author.

ISBN 979-8-9852374-6-7

CHB MEDIA, PUBLISHER

(386) 957-4761

chbmedia@gmail.com

www.chbbooks.com

First Edition

Printed in the USA

Illustrations by David Lawter

Design by CHB Media

Dedication

To my recently departed father,
the music teacher; for both my parents,
Sal and Judy, lovers of Cats and Music.

And thank you to our beloved
pet cat Tooney, for sharing her
long and magical life with us.

It is my wish that this book inspire
both young and older minds
to explore the wonders of music.

This is Tooney the cat.

Tooney is a baby kitten.
She is only eight weeks old.

She is so tiny she can fit
in the palm of your hand.

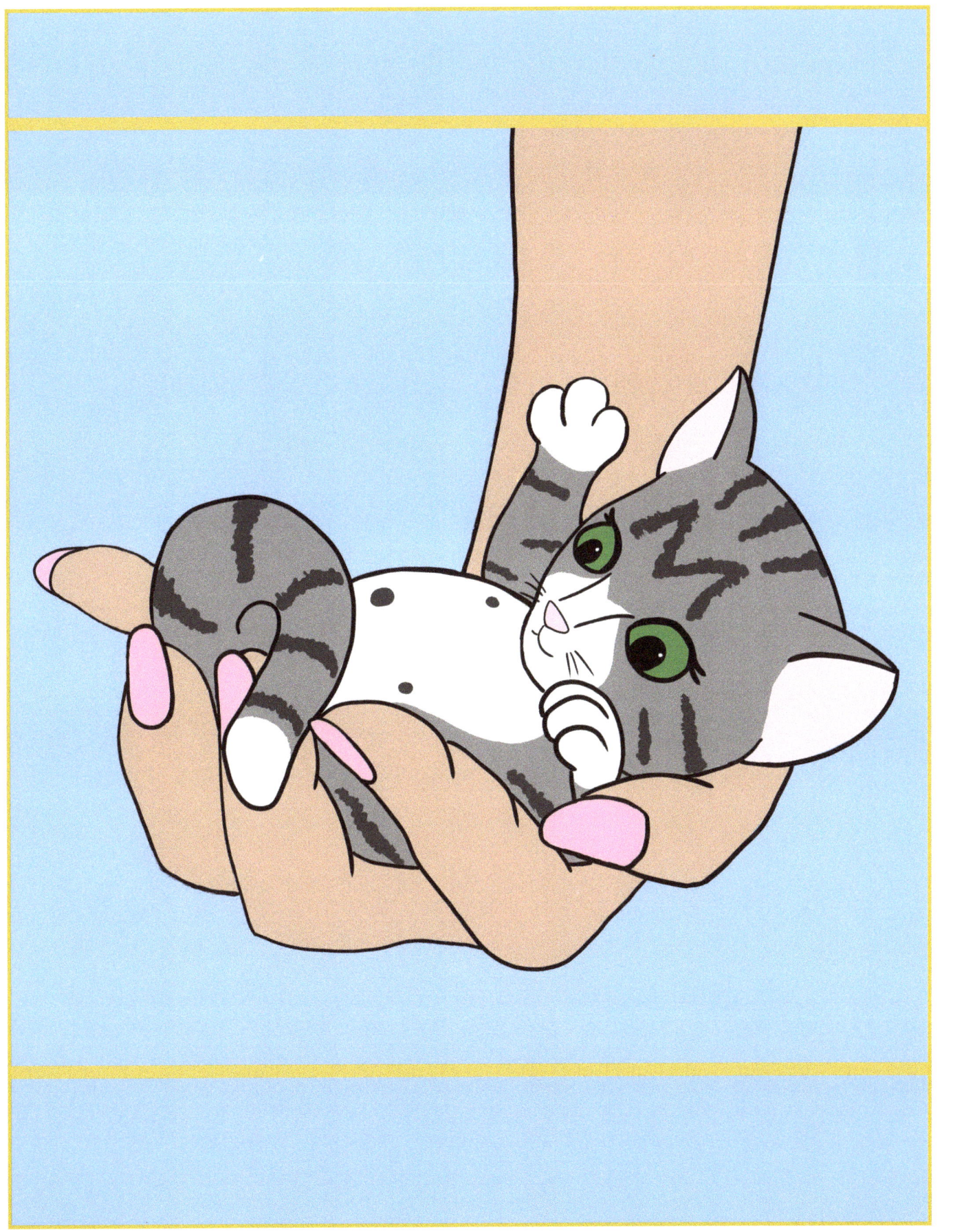

Tooney lives with Jim and Michelle,
who have a music studio in their home.

When Jim wants to see
how much Tooney weighs,
he puts her on a postage scale.

"A whopping two pounds," laughs Jim.

Little Tooney can hide
in very small places
where bigger cats cannot.

She can run and jump and climb
just like a big cat.

Tooney can jump and climb up on
almost all the furniture in the house,
but she is too small to jump on
the high table in the living room.

Instead, Tooney sits under the table and watches all the things that go on in that big room.

Often, music fills the house from many musical instruments in Jim and Michelle's music studio.

One day a boy came over and blew into a trombone.

The sound was so loud that it scared Tooney. She scurried out from under the table and ran away.

As time went on, Tooney
grew to love music.

When it was time for a nap
Michelle would put on
soft, pretty music.

Tooney would stretch out, give
a big kitty yawn and fall asleep.

Other times there would be lively music on the radio and she would run and hop to the music.

Every day Tooney sits on a chair in the shop and watches Jim fix the instruments.

Sometimes Jim plays the instruments to test them. One time Tooney sat on Jim's knee as he played a flute. The sweet sounds of the flute lulled her to sleep.

When she's not watching Jim, Tooney likes to walk through the jungle of instrument cases. She peeks inside at all the different instruments.

She sees big instruments like the trombone and saxophone. And smaller instruments like the flute and clarinet.

Some instruments are shiny and brassy. Some are silver.

Some instruments have a few buttons. Others have lots of keys and buttons.

Tooney likes to rest under the table.

When the children come by,
Tooney listens to the different sounds
they make with their instruments.

She likes to visit with the children.
Sometimes they hold her.
Then they leave, carrying their
new instrument in their hand.

Oh how Tooney wishes she too could play an instrument. Sometimes when Michelle and Jim go out, they leave some of the instruments on the floor.

Tooney taps some of the buttons and valves with her paw.
No sound comes out.

She even sticks her tiny head
inside the bell of the trumpet,
but she still can't find the music.

So the weeks go by and Tooney watches the parade of children with their instruments.

And she sits and watches Jim repair the instruments.

And she dances and plays to the frisky music, or curls up and naps to the pretty songs on the radio.

And as time passed, Tooney grew bigger and bigger.

Until one day she had grown big enough to jump up on that high table in the living room. And do you know what she found? That table was not really a table, but a beautiful piano.

And when she walked and danced across the keys of the piano, she made music! Finally, Tooney found an instrument she could play!

Now when the children come to the studio, Tooney plays the piano for them.

And when the children leave with their instruments, Tooney no longer feels sad, because now she too can make music!

ILLUSTRATOR DAVID LAWTER

David Lawter works as a freelance illustrator and animator for television, web sites, planetarium laser shows, and original cartoons. When he's not drawing or working as an animator, he pursues his other passion: playing upright bass and performing professionally in the genres of classical, musical theatre, and jazz. He spends time in New Smyrna Beach, Florida, and Asheville, North Carolina.

www.ingramcontent.com/pod-product-compliance
Lightning Source LLC
LaVergne TN
LVHW070602070526
838199LV00011B/468